PuzzleMania®
Summer Puzzles

HIGHLIGHTS PRESS
Honesdale, Pennsylvania

CONTENTS

When you finish a puzzle, check it off √.
Good luck, and happy puzzling!

Wordplay

Do the Math

A-Mazing!

Hidden Pictures®

Look Twice

Brainteasers

Summer Q's

Log Jamming

Start

Grab your wetsuit! This log is about to take the plunge. Can you steer it smoothly all the way to **FINISH** without getting soaked? Just one path will take you there.

Illustrated by Steve Skelton

Finish

Hidden Pictures® Dog Wash

There's more than meets the eye at this dog wash. Can you find the hidden objects?

turtle

bell

book

mug

boomerang

ice-cream cone

whistle

fish

ring

spoon

ruler

banana

mallet

light bulb

baseball

canoe

comb

pencil

fishhook

hockey stick

Up the Creek

The Roaring River Run is on! This year the paddlers can pick up points as they make their way upriver. Add the points in each lane to find out who racks up the highest score.

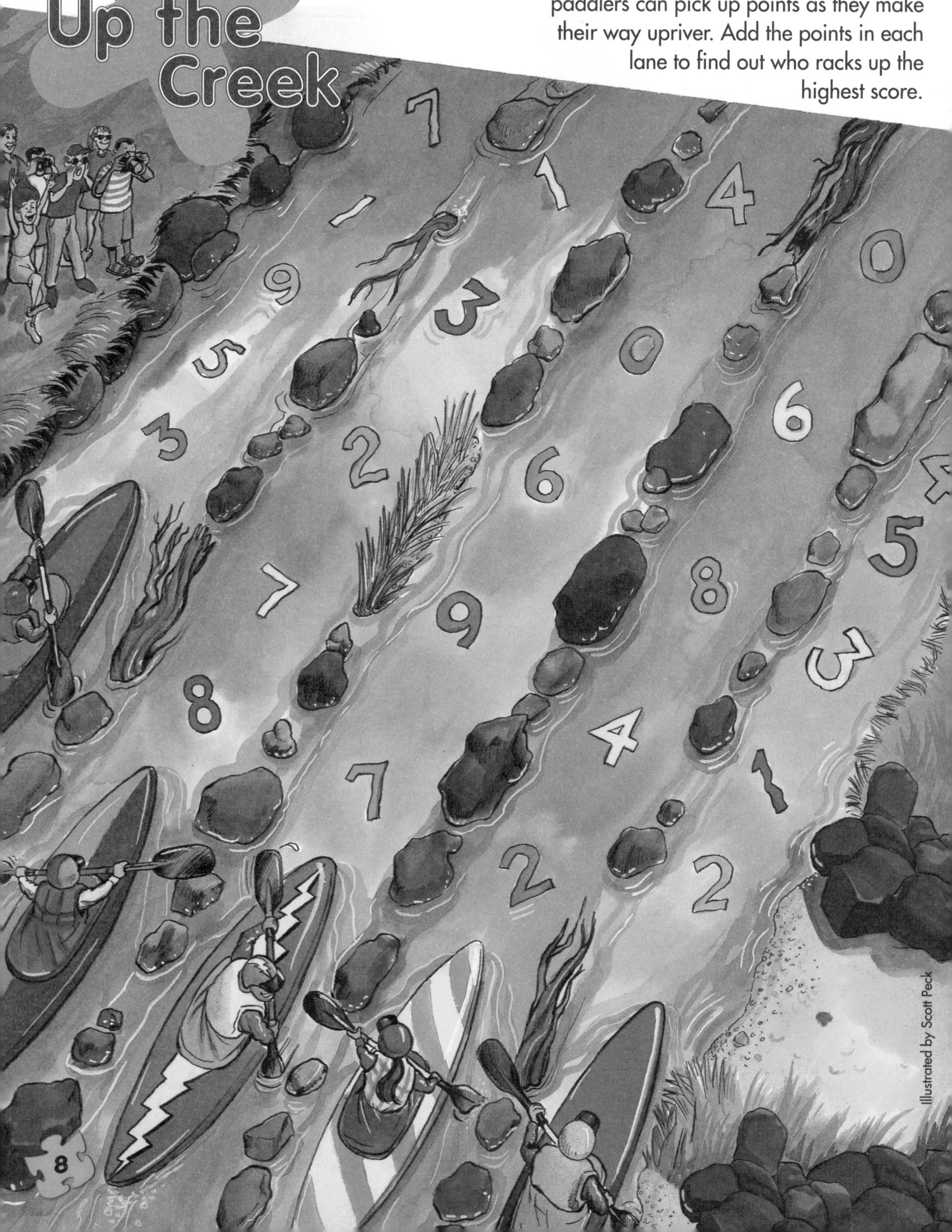

7
1
1
4
9
0
3
5
3
2
6
3
6
0
7
7
9
6
8
8
5
7
9
4
3
8
4
1
7
2
2
2

Back to the Grind

We've flipped **20** skateboard tricks into this grid. They are hidden up, down, across, backwards, and diagonally. Get on board and see how many you can find.

Word List

- ~~AIRWALK~~
- BACKFLIP
- BIGFLIP
- BOARDSLIDE
- BUTTERFLIP
- CASPER
- DAFFY
- HEELFLIP
- HELIPOP
- INDY
- LIPSLIDE
- MANUAL
- MCTWIST
- NOLLIE
- NOSEGRIND
- POGO
- RAILSTAND
- SMITH GRIND
- SPACEWALK
- SUGARCANE

```
P Y B M A N U A L L
P I A I R W A L K I
S B L P G Y D N I K
K O D F F F F S K K
A A N F L J L M I K
T R A B Y E W I T S
E D T E Z N E T H P
I S S D M F S H G A
B L L I C D U G R C
U I I L T N G R I E
T D A S W I A I N W
T E R P I R R N A A
E D I I S G C D L L
R E Y L T E A S K K
F C O O L S N C C C
L K G E U O E B A A
I O W R W N N T S S
P H H E L I P O P P
B A C K F L I P E E
Z W H E E L S R R R
```

Puzzle by Amie Jane Leavitt

Illustrated by Garry Colby

Kite Plight

Hang on tight! These kite flyers have gotten their strings tangled. Follow each person's string to find out which kite he or she is flying.

Illustrated by Brian White

11

Camp Out

Cole and each of his three friends went to a different camp this summer. Each camp had a different theme, and each was held at a different time. From the clues below, can you figure out which camp each friend attended and when?

Use the chart to keep track of your answers. Put an **X** in each box that can't be true and an **O** in boxes that match.

	Cole	Abby	Marissa	Paul
Music Camp				
Soccer Camp				
Swimming Camp				
Art Camp				
July 1–15				
July 16–31				
August 1–15				
August 16–31				

1. Cole's camp did not have a single soccer ball. He went to camp sometime in August.

2. The girl who went to Art Camp was there from July 16 to July 31.

3. Paul's camp was all about music. He did not go in August.

4. Marissa went to her camp before Abby went to hers. Abby was not the last friend to go to camp.

Hidden Pictures® Paddle Pals

sock

saltshaker

mug

umbrella

artist's brush

cane

pennant

heart

fishhook

pencil

whistle

puzzle piece

ruler

slice of pizza

ladle

palm tree

snowman

ice pop

open book

stamp

mushroom

Illustrated by Jennifer Harney

13

Ring the Bell

You can help Marcus ring the bell at the state fair. For each question, circle the answer listed under **A**, **B**, or **C**. Then shade in a square on the matching column on the carnival bell ringer. As you do, the boxes will climb to the top and one will ring the bell. We've filled in one square to get you started.

Which is . . .	A	B	C
1. a shade of blue?	azure	scarlet	olive
2. the capital of New York?	New York City	Syracuse	Albany
3. the number of stripes on the U.S. flag?	50	25	13
4. the Spanish word for cat?	perro	gato	danza
5. the month when spring starts?	March	April	May
6. a baker's dozen?	11	12	13
7. a group of whales?	swarm	pod	army
8. an Asian country?	Thailand	Chile	Tanzania
9. the smallest amount?	1 teaspoon	1 tablespoon	1 cup
10. the opposite of timid?	scared	outgoing	shy
11. the shape of a stop sign?	circle	octagon	hexagon
12. a reptile?	newt	guppy	iguana
13. the number of periods in a hockey game?	3	4	5
14. Hawaii's ocean?	Atlantic	Indian	Pacific
15. equal to 11 x 11?	101	111	121
16. a brass instrument?	trumpet	clarinet	cello
17. a chess piece?	prince	queen	princess
18. the Grand Canyon state?	Texas	Idaho	Arizona
19. equal to 5 yards?	15 feet	10 feet	20 feet
20. a flightless bird?	emu	stork	duck

A B C

Sun and Shades

It's a perfect day for the beach—and for trying out those new sunglasses! Shade your eyes and look carefully. There are **five pairs** of sunglasses that match exactly. Can you find them all?

Illustrated by Genevieve Kote

17

Sailing Sums

I's time for the regatta. In order for each yacht to score points, it must sail around all of the buoys that are the same

8 2 3 5 1 7 6 5 4 7 5 8

color as its hull. The yacht with the highest score wins the race. Can you figure out which boat will sail to victory?

Hidden Pictures®
Superchallenge!

There are **30** objects hidden in this river scene. Without clues or knowing what to look for, try to find them all. Good luck!

Illustrated by Paula Becker

Double Dips

Ike's Ice-Cream Parlor is packed today. While everyone eats a treat, see if you can find at least **20** differences between these pictures.

Illustrated by Peter Grosshauser

Can you find 8 scoops of mint-chocolate-chip ice cream on these two pages?

It's Campy

Use the clues to fill in the answers in this crossword puzzle. Every answer has something to do with camping. We did one to get you started.

Across

5. A bottle or canteen holds this.

7. These hold up the tent.

8. Masked animals that come out at night

10. Make a wish on these.

11. A walk through the woods

13. Carry your supplies in this.

15. These birds are awake at night.

18. This keeps mosquitoes away.

19. You might wear these on an 11 Across.

20. Put this in a cooler to chill food.

21. Bring your rod and reel for this.

22. Treats made from marshmallows, chocolate, and graham crackers

Down

1. Gather this for a fire

2. A lunar night light

3. Camping shelter

4. Carry this to see at night

6. Animal footprints

9. Your camping "bed"

10. Slide marshmallows onto this for roasting.

12. Small, narrow boat

14. You might cook hot dogs over this.

16. What you tell around a 14 Down.

17. You might go swimming here.

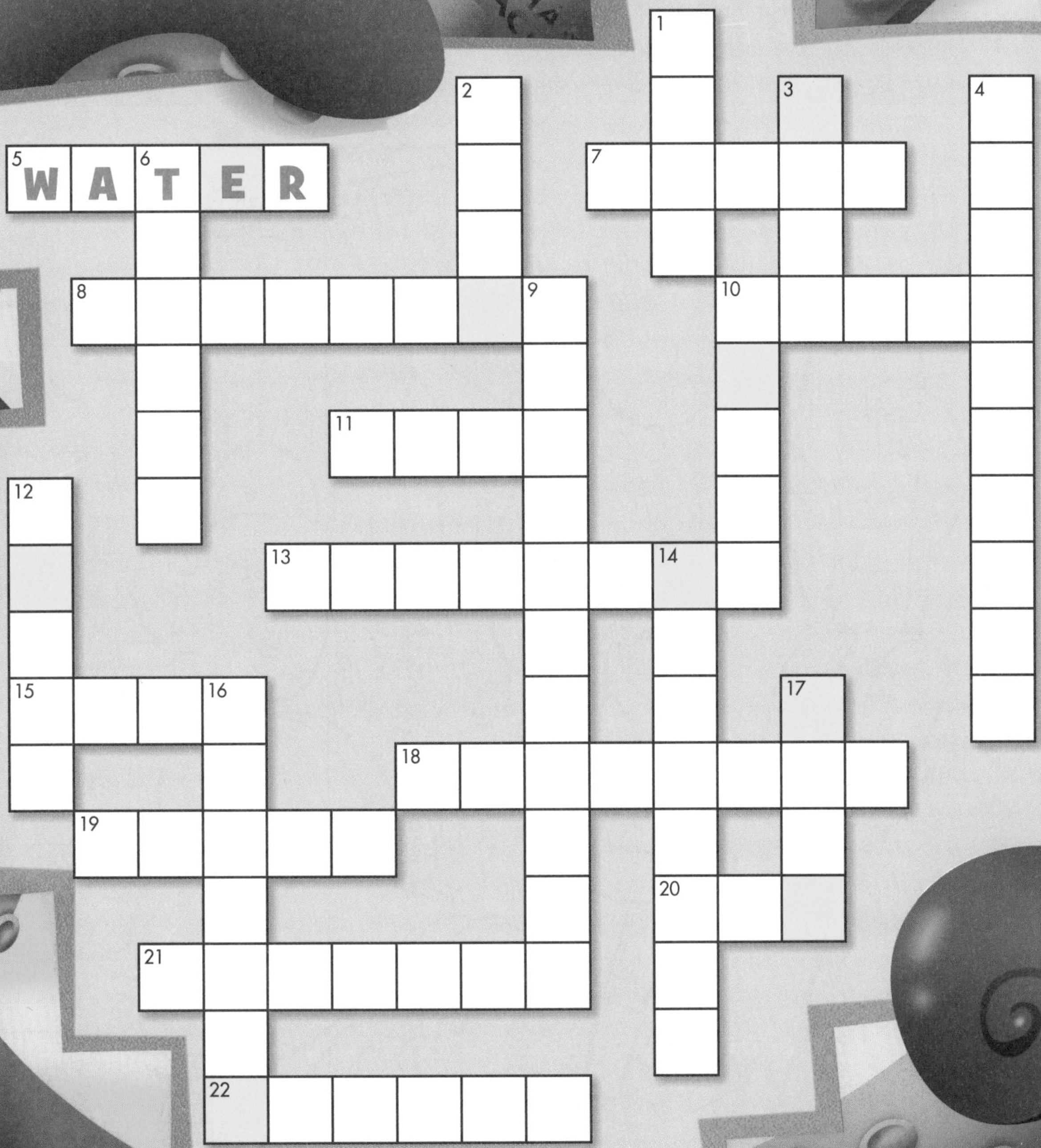

Bonus Puzzle

After you finish the crossword, fill in the shaded squares in order from top to bottom and left to right to see the answer to this riddle:

What do octopuses take on camping trips?

☐☐☐☐-☐☐☐☐☐

Puzzle by Shannon Caster

Illustrated by Peter Grosshauser

Hidden Pictures®
This Way, Hikers!

magnifying glass

fork

worm

pencil

mushroom

slice of bread

key

heart

drinking glass with straw

banana

book

wastebasket

26

feather

mitten

artist's brush

toothbrush

carrot

pushpin

ice-cream cone

rabbit

snowman

wedge of lemon

Illustrated by Jennifer Harney

Tic Tac Row

Each of these ice-cream treats has something in common with the other two treats in the same row. For example, in the top row across, all three treats have whipped cream. Look at the other rows across, down, and diagonally. Can you tell what's alike in each row?

Rafting Record

These adventurers are about to set off on a rafting trip. Each raft holds 4 guests and 1 guide. Maritza (holding the clipboard) is not going on the trip; she's keeping a list of all the expenses so she can organize a similar trip next year. Can you help her by filling in the blanks below? (Here's a hint: There are 14 guests going on the rafting trip.)

Cost per person if raft is not full: $27.50
Cost per full raft: $105.00 (4 people)
Paddle rental: $4.50 • Life jacket rental: $6.00

1. Total number of rafts needed for this group: _____

2. Total cost of the raft rental for this group: _____

3. Every guest is renting a paddle.
   Total number of paddles needed: _____

4. Total cost of the paddle rental for this group: _____

5. Katie, Kevin, and the Kline triplets brought their own life jackets. Total cost of the life jacket rental for the rest of the group: _____

6. Combined total of all charges for this group: _____

7. Total number of guides needed for this group: _____

Illustrated by Scott Peck

29

Hidden Pictures®
Tents Up!

apple

envelope

kite

oven mitt

pineapple

carrot

slice of pie

button

pencil

ruler

This scene has many wild things to look for. Can you find the hidden objects?

pennant

paintbrush

horseshoe

top hat

spool of thread

arrow

banana

Illustrated by Rocky Fuller

trowel

wristwatch

mushroom

spoon

Hidden WORDS

There are six words (not pictures!) hidden in the scene below.
Can you find **CANDY, GAMES, PRIZE, RIDE, TICKETS,** and **WIN?**

Illustrated by Kelly Kennedy

Spotted Sums

On Monday, Sharona spotted 5 swallows. Every day, the number of swallows she sees doubles. She sees 10 swallows on Tuesday, which is double the number she saw on Monday, and 20 on Wednesday. Fill out the rest of her chart. On what day does Sharona see more than 600 swallows?

Week 1		Week 2	
Monday	**5**		
Tuesday	___	Monday	___
Wednesday	___	Tuesday	___
Thursday	___	Wednesday	___
Friday	___	Thursday	___
Saturday	___	Friday	___
Sunday	___	Saturday	___
		Sunday	___

33

Beach Q's

Beach Reach

Can you help Sandy find her way back to her beach towel?

Start

Finish

Illustrated by Mike Moran

Missing Vowels

BCH NMLS are the words *beach animals* with the vowels taken away. Can you figure out the names of the bch nmls below?

_____
CRB

_____
CLM

_____
SGLL

_____
PLCN

_____
S STR

A Shore Thing

Match each of these U.S. beaches to its state.

Waikiki Beach •   • California

Palm Beach •   • Florida

Venice Beach •   • Hawaii

Cape Hatteras •   • Massachusetts

Cape Cod •   • North Carolina

Sand Castle Contest

It's time to dig in and design a sand sculpture for the big contest. Draw yours here.

Shell Match

Which two seashells match exactly?

A

B

C

D

JUMBLed BEacH

Unscramble each set of letters to get the name of something you might bring to the beach.

LALB — — — —

KOBO — — — —

WELTO — — — — —

LANDSAS — — — — — — —

EGOBIO DABOR — — — — — — — — —

— — — —

GLUSSANESS — — — — — — — — —

Hidden Pictures®
Leaping Lemonade!

wedge of lime

shoe

open book

shorts

ice-cream cone

heart

snake

sailboat

artist's brush

glove

teacup

pencil

needle

ring

turtle

36

Tic Tac Row

What do the kids in each row (across, down, and diagonally) have in common?

Illustrated by Scott Angle

Fair Play

Every summer, Loopy Lane holds a street fair. There are some strange sights this year. Can you find at least **25** odd, weird, or silly things in this picture?

WACKY WAY

LOOPY LANE

39

Treasure Hunt

Captain Platinum keeps his treasure on a secret island. To find out what the treasure is, **start at the Computer Keys**. Follow the directions on the map to go from island to island. When you find a letter, stash it away in the ship's locker. Once you reach Treasure Island, the letters will tell you what the captain keeps there.

Coney Island
Take a **D** and sail to Gritty Island.

Itchy Island
Mosquitoes! Go east.

Sail on Northeast

Treasure Island

Kite Island
Fly north to Itchy Island.

Take an **H**. Go northeast to Treasure Island.
Cat Island

N
W   E
S

START
Computer Keys
System error. Go east.

Angle Island
Go east to a fruity isle.

40

Gritty Island Nothing but sand. Sail east.

Go west, young sailor.

Fan Island Pick up an **F**. Sail south.

Spagetti Island Take an **I** and go to Hammer Island.

Tail Island Swing east.

Palm Island Stay east.

Go west to Cat Island. **Pirate Island**

Take an **S** and go to Pirate Island.

Sunny Island Load an **G** and go to Arrow Island.

Point Island Go west to Kite Island.

Hammer Island

Lolli Island Pick up an **I**. Sail to Point Island.

Letter Island Load **G**. Sail to Angle Island.

Arrow Island Go west.

Peel north to Sunny Island. **Banana Island**

Illustrated by Terry Taylor

41

Illustrated by Mike Moran

slice of
pizza

horseshoe

hourglass

cane

heart

yo-yo

dustpan

screwdriver

belt

boat

key

flashlight

crescent
moon

dinosaur

plate

Croquet Cross

Find the hidden objects in the croquet game on the left. Then fill in the ball puzzle with words from the WORD LIST on this page. Use the number of letters in each word as a clue to where it might fit. We filled in one word to get you started.

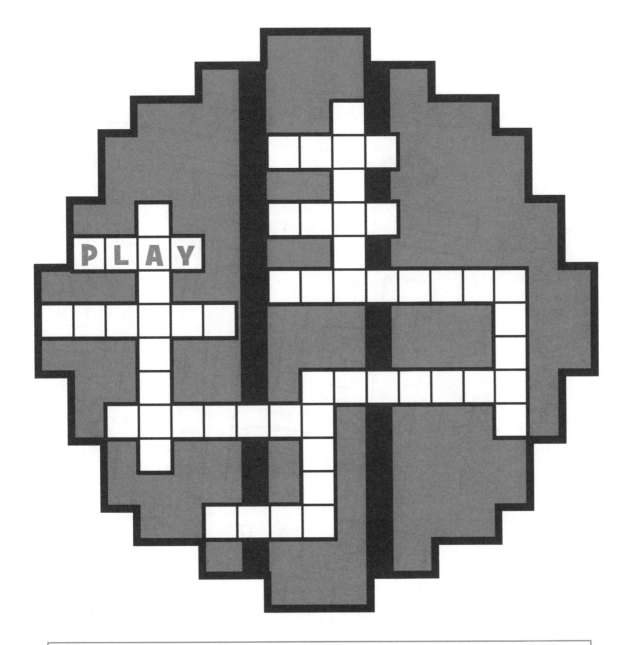

WORD LIST

4 LETTERS
BALL
GAME
PLAY
TEAM

5 LETTERS
SCORE
STAKE

6 LETTERS
MALLET
WICKET

7 LETTERS
CROQUET
STRIKER

8 LETTERS
BACKYARD
OUTDOORS

Bottled Up

Ella found a bottle washed up on the beach. It has a secret riddle message inside! To find the answer to the riddle, first find the one path from **START** to **FINISH**. Then write the letters you find along the way in the spaces below.

What's the best place to dance at the beach?

Finish

Illustrated by David Coulson

Illustrated by Daryll Collins

There is more than meets the eye at this hot dog stand. Can you find the hidden objects?

beehive

slice of pizza

envelope

doughnut

candy cane

boomerang

golf club

button

comb

pencil

slice of orange

snake

top hat

seashell

carrot

magic wand

jump rope

sock

musical note

ruler

47

Park Here

The United States has dozens of national parks. The names of 33 are hidden in these letters. Can you find them all? They are hidden up, down, across, backwards, and diagonally. (The state abbreviations are not hidden.)

Word List

ACADIA (ME)
ARCHES (UT)
BADLANDS (SD)
BIG BEND (TX)
BISCAYNE (FL)
CONGAREE (SC)
CRATER LAKE (OR)
DENALI (AK)
DRY TORTUGAS (FL)
EVERGLADES (FL)
GLACIER BAY (AK)
GRAND CANYON (AZ)
GRAND TETON (WY)
GREAT BASIN (NV)
HALEAKALA (HI)
HOT SPRINGS (AR)

ISLE ROYALE (MI)
JOSHUA TREE (CA)
KATMAI (AK)
MAMMOTH CAVE (KY)
MESA VERDE (CO)
MOUNT RAINIER (WA)
OLYMPIC (WA)
REDWOOD (CA)
ROCKY MOUNTAIN (CO)
SAGUARO (AZ)
SEQUOIA (CA)
SHENANDOAH (VA)
WIND CAVE (SD)
YELLOWSTONE (ID, MT, WY)
YOSEMITE (CA)
ZION (UT)

GREAT SMOKY MOUNTAINS (NC, TN)

```
S Z N G R A N D C A N Y O N E S M
N I P M O U N T R A I N I E R N A
O O R O R T E L A Y O R E L S I M
Y N D R Y T O R T U G A S Y N A M
R O S A L A K A E L A H G E G T O
O W S E D A L G R E V E A L R N T
C C I E D E N A L I E G J L E U H
K K O N M A T R A P N R O O A O C
Y E R N D I S D K B Y I C W T M A
M R S T G C T E E I A X I S B Y V
O J K L Z A A E F G C Y P T A K E
U I O V O I R V S B S R M O S O B
N A J S D U R E E E I S Y N I M A
T M E A H E Q J E N B G L E N S D
A T C G D U C D G D B J O Q Z T L
I A N W O R A S A G U A R O B A A
N K O I A N O T E T D N A R G E N
X O A B V Y A B R E I C A L G R D
D Y H A O D N A N E H S S I V G S
M E S A V E R D E S E H C R A O B
```

49

Fore!

Patty and her pals played a round of miniature golf. Now it's time to figure out who won. Add up the scores of

1
Patty: 3
Paula: 4
Pete: 2
Perry: 6

4
Patty: 6
Paula: 1
Pete: 5
Perry: 2

2
Patty: 4
Paula: 2
Pete: 3
Perry: 1

3
Patty: 5
Paula: 3
Pete: 6
Perry: 4

6
Patty: 1
Paula: 6
Pete: 4
Perry: 5

15
Patty: 1
Paula: 6
Pete: 5
Perry: 1

5
Patty: 2
Paula: 5
Pete: 1
Perry: 3

each golfer to find the
champion. Remember, in
golf, the lowest score wins.

11
Patty: 1
Paula: 2
Pete: 4
Perry: 5

12
Patty: 6
Paula: 1
Pete: 3
Perry: 3

13
Patty: 2
Paula: 4
Pete: 1
Perry: 5

9
Patty: 2
Paula: 3
Pete: 2
Perry: 1

10
Patty: 5
Paula: 5
Pete: 3
Perry: 4

7

8
Patty: 4
Paula: 1
Pete: 5
Perry: 3

Patty: 3
Paula: 4
Pete: 1
Perry: 2

14
Patty: 3
Paula: 5
Pete: 6
Perry: 4

18
Patty: 4
Paula: 1
Pete: 2
Perry: 3

17
Patty: 4
Paula: 3
Pete: 4
Perry: 2

16
Patty: 5
Paula: 2
Pete: 2
Perry: 6

FINISH

Moonlighting

Trevor and his family took a hike in the moonlight. Now they need help finding the way back to their campsite. Can you find the path that will take them to their tents?

Start

Finish

Hidden Pictures®
What a Catch!

slice of pie

muffin

carrot

glove

banana

candle

tack

bell

envelope

artist's brush

pencil

chicken

candy corn

lamp

ballpoint pen

mitten

slice of pizza

toothbrush

butter knife

Illustrated By Chuck Dillon

53

Parrot Pairs

Each parrot in this picture has one that looks exactly like it.
Can you find each matching pair?

Hidden Pictures® Grab a Board

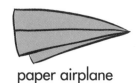 paper airplane

teacup

envelope

lollipop

hat

dog bone

 bat

spoon

tack

 slice of pizza

 flashlight

 candy cane

 mallet

 ladder

 spatula

Surf Cross

Find the hidden objects in the beach scene on the left. Then fill in the surfboard puzzle with words from the WORD LIST on this page. Use the number of letters in each word as a clue to where it might fit. We filled in one word to get you started.

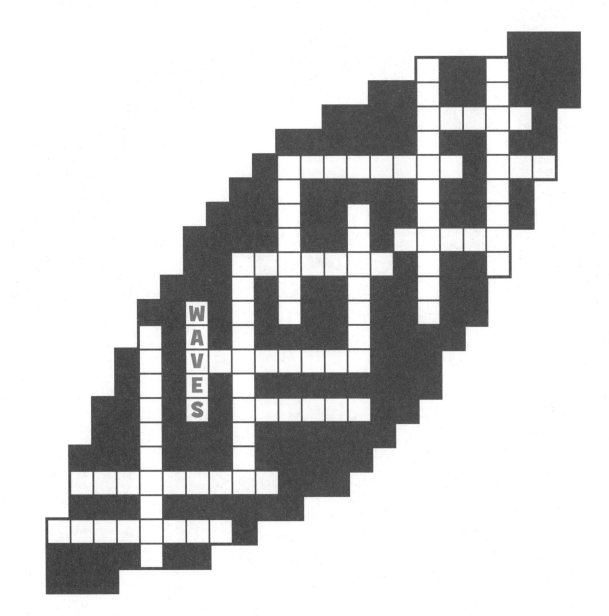

WORD LIST

3 LETTERS
HOT

5 LETTERS
OCEAN
TOWEL
~~WAVES~~

6 LETTERS
SHOVEL

7 LETTERS
DOLPHIN
SANDALS
SEAGULL

8 LETTERS
SWIMSUIT
UMBRELLA
VACATION

9 LETTERS
BEACH BALL
SUNSCREEN

10 LETTERS
SANDCASTLE
SUNGLASSES

11 LETTERS
BOOGIE BOARD

Battle of the Bands

The band is playing their big hit, "Double Trouble." Before they finish, see if you can find **20** differences between these pictures.

Which instrument does not appear on either page?

- ✶ guitar
- ✶ tambourine
- ✶ keyboard
- ✶ drum

Road Trip

Wanda and Rhonda are planning cross-country trips. They will both start in Los Angeles, California, and end in Washington, D.C. However, the roads they take and cities

WANDA'S WAY

START

Los Angeles

San Diego

Phoenix

El Paso

Amarillo

Dallas

New Orleans

Birmingham

Atlanta

Knoxville

Washington, D.C.

RHONDA'S ROUTE

START

Los Angeles

Las Vegas

Salt Lake City

Denver

Oakley

Kansas City

Chicago

Indianapolis

Cincinnati

Charleston

Washington, D.C.

Illustrated by John Nez

Salt Lake City

495

486

Denver

375

Las Vegas

Los Angeles

124

San Diego

350

Phoenix

42

437

El Pa

they visit will be very different. Add up each girl's miles from one city to the next. When they reach Washington, D.C., will Wanda or Rhonda have traveled more miles?

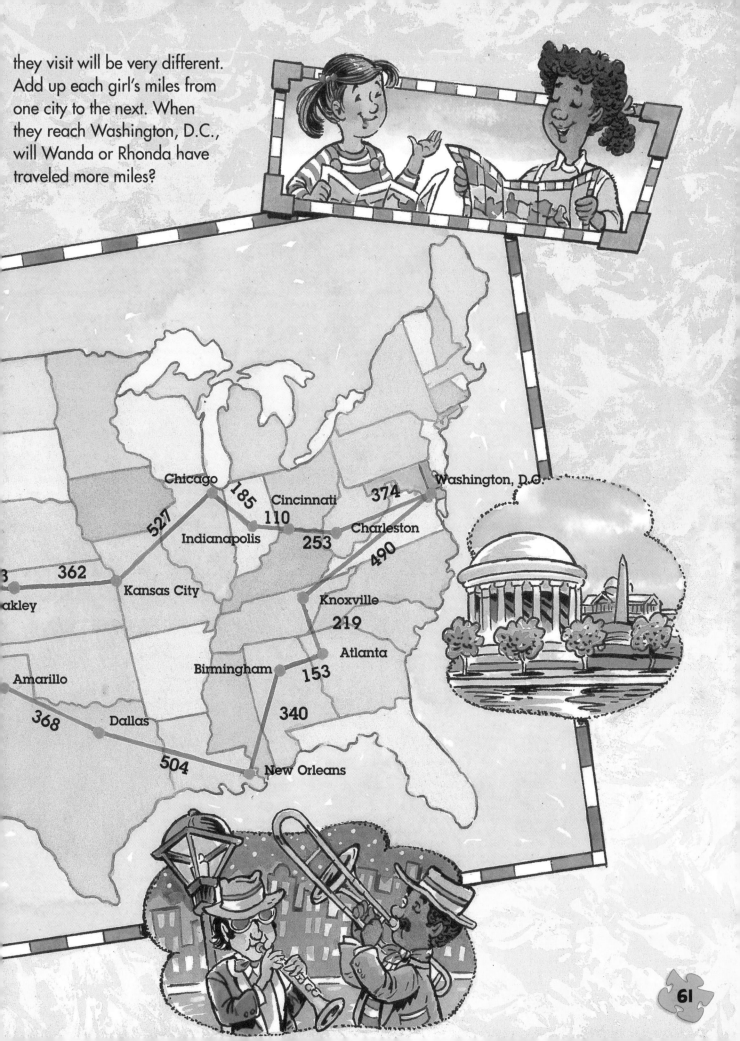

Chicago 185 Cincinnati 374 Washington, D.C.
527 110
Indianapolis 253 Charleston
362 490
Kansas City Knoxville
219
Atlanta
Birmingham 153
340
Amarillo
368
Dallas
504 New Orleans

Hidden Pictures® Superchallenge!

There are **30** objects hidden on this beach. Without clues or knowing what to look for, try to find them all. Good luck!

SNACKS

Illustrated by Paula Becker

Park Maze

START

64

Can you help Mike and Mia meet up with their friends?
Find a clear path from START to FINISH.

FUN HOUSE

Illustrated by Steve Skelton

FINISH

Skate Q's

Get Rolling

Katie is racing to the finish line. Which place will she get?

Start

Illustrated by Mike Moran

Hockey or Figure?

Some of these terms come from **ice hockey** and others from **figure skating**. Can you figure out which belong to which sport?

SLAP SHOT	**H**	**F**
DOUBLE AXEL	**H**	**F**
ICING	**H**	**F**
TOE JUMP	**H**	**F**
LUTZ	**H**	**F**
FACEOFF	**H**	**F**
HAT TRICK	**H**	**F**
SALCHOW	**H**	**F**
DEATH SPIRAL	**H**	**F**
POWER PLAY	**H**	**F**

Trick or Not?

Each pair of terms has one in-line skate trick and one faker. Can you tell which terms are the real tricks?

Back Flip or Front Trip

Swing Set or Front Slide

Royale Grind or Rye Grinder

Mute Grab or Jute Bag

Grape Juice or Grapevine

Barrel Roll or Monkey Barrel

66

ROLLER Twins

Which two in-line skates are exactly alike?

NeW Jersey

Your hockey team needs new uniforms.
Design your dream jersey here!

Joking Around

Why can't you tell a joke while ice skating? To see the answer, write each set of colored letters on the lines at the right.

TIMHCCIERGUAEHCTPK

GREEN _____

BLUE _____

RED _____

PURPLE _____

BLACK _____

67

Fork it Over

It's almost time to eat! But where are the forks? They're here, if you know where to look. Take a closer look. There are **20** forks hidden in the scene. How many can you find?

Illustrated by Kevin Rechin

Here Comes the Sun!

Grab your sunglasses! We've hidden **35** words or phrases that contain the letters SUN in this grid. Each time SUN appears in a word, it is replaced by a ☀. Look up, down, across, backwards, and diagonally to find the words. If you can find them all, you are a star!

Word List

~~MIDNIGHT SUN~~
SUNBATHE
SUNBEAM
SUN BEAR
SUNBELT
SUNBLOCK
SUNBONNET
SUNBURN
SUNBURST
SUNDAE
SUN DANCE
SUNDAY
SUNDEW
SUNDIAL
SUNDOWN
SUNDRESS
SUNFISH
SUNFLOWER
SUNGLASSES
SUNHAT
SUNLAMP
SUNLIGHT
SUNNY-SIDE-UP
SUNPORCH
SUNRISE
SUNROOF
SUNSCREEN
SUNSEEKER
SUNSET
SUNSHINE
SUNSPOT
SUNSTROKE
SUNSUIT
SUNTAN
SUNUP

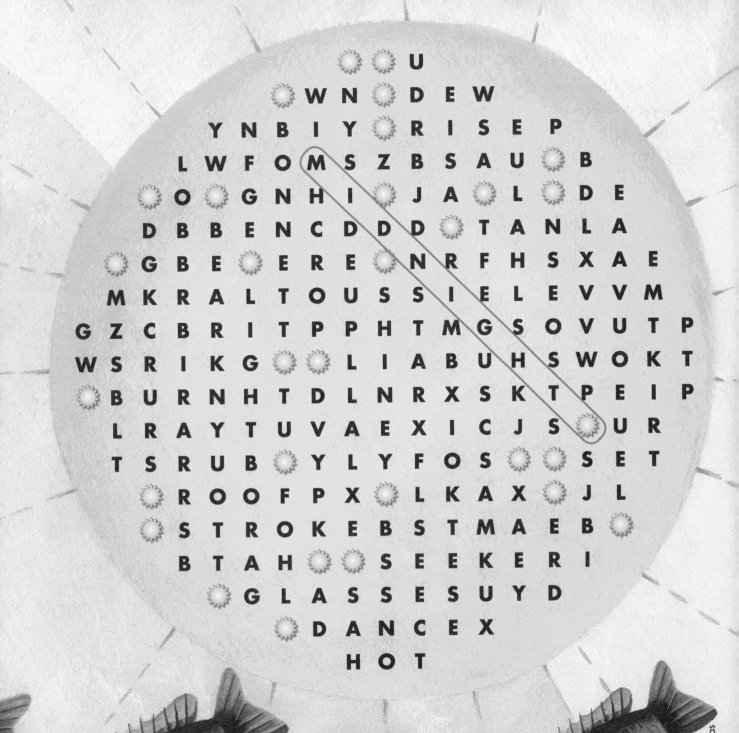

Hooked!

Everyone has caught something. But what? Follow each person's fishing line to find out what he or she snagged.

Hidden WORDS

There are six words (not pictures!) hidden in the scene below.
Can you find **BAIT, CANOE, HOOK, MOUNTAIN, NET,** and **PINE**?

Illustrated by Kelly Kennedy

Phone Age

Before leaving summer camp, Jed and some of his camp mates exchanged cell phone numbers. (They all had the same area code.) As he was riding home, Jed noticed an odd coincidence. The digits in each camper's phone number added up to his or her age. Can you match the cell phone numbers to the campers?

Sylvia, age 14
Oliver, age 15
Jaime, age 7
Lara, age 8
Ari, age 11
Bruce, age 12
Lola, age 9
Joel, age 16
Nate, age 10
Ellis, age 13

802-1005
521-0600
233-1202
410-2102
203-0002
310-0050
202-4000
614-3001
321-1103
401-3121

Illustrated by Bill Colrus

75

Just Beachy

This crossword is like a day at the beach. Every answer in this puzzle is made up of letters from the phrase

BEACH UMBRELLAS.

We've put the first one in place for you. Can you stake out the rest?

Across

1. Hermit or fiddler
3. Sky, indigo, or navy
5. A bundle of hay
6. Can be thrown as a slider or a sinker
10. BBQ is short for this.
11. It might wake you up.
12. Money
15. Snap a picture with this.
17. Ice-_____ cone
19. Aggies, tigers, and cat's eyes
20. A painting stand
22. Remove a pencil mark
23. Breakfast or dinner
25. Basement
26. One of the five senses

Down

1. Breakfast food
2. They straighten teeth.
4. A snakelike fish
5. A comb's partner
7. Sit on these at the ballpark.
8. Walk a dog with this.
9. St. Patrick's Day month
13. _____ hoop
14. Spaghetti topper
15. A 3-D square
16. A measure of land
18. Spread this around garden plants.
19. Bicep or tricep
21. On a _____ of 1 to 10
23. The red planet
24. Mary had a little one.

CRAB

Illustrated by Peter Grosshauser

Digit Does It

That amazing investigator, Inspector Digit, is hot on the trail of an ice-cream crook. Someone took all the cones from Softee's Sweets.

Illustrated by Joe Boddy

The only clue is a coded note. Can you decipher the note, find the clues, and help the inspector lick this case? The first line reads, **"Dear Inspector Digit."**

$\overline{11}\,\overline{4}\,\overline{5}\,\overline{15}$ $\overline{3}\,\overline{8}\,\overline{18}\,\overline{13}\,\overline{4}\,\overline{10}\,\overline{7}\,\overline{2}\,\overline{15}$ $\overline{11}\,\overline{3}\,\overline{20}\,\overline{3}\,\overline{7}{}'$

$\overline{18}\,\overline{2}$ $\overline{7}\,\overline{9}\,\overline{4}\,\overline{6}$ $\overline{18}\,\overline{4}\,\overline{8}\,\overline{7}$ $\overline{7}\,\overline{9}\,\overline{4}$

$\overline{10}\,\overline{15}\,\overline{4}\,\overline{5}\,\overline{19}$ $\overline{2}\,\overline{17}$ $\overline{7}\,\overline{9}\,\overline{4}$ $\overline{10}\,\overline{2}\,\overline{13}\,\overline{18}$

$\overline{5}\,\overline{17}\,\overline{7}\,\overline{4}\,\overline{15}$ $\overline{19}\,\overline{4}$ $\overline{9}\,\overline{2}\,\overline{22}$ $\overline{18}\,\overline{22}\,\overline{4}\,\overline{4}\,\overline{7}.$

$\overline{21}\,\overline{1}\,\overline{7}$ $\overline{19}\,\overline{6}$ $\overline{7}\,\overline{15}\,\overline{5}\,\overline{3}\,\overline{16}$ $\overline{22}\,\overline{3}\,\overline{16}\,\overline{16}$ $\overline{21}\,\overline{4}$

$\overline{10}\,\overline{2}\,\overline{16}\,\overline{11}$ $\overline{21}\,\overline{4}\,\overline{17}\,\overline{2}\,\overline{15}\,\overline{4}$ $\overline{6}\,\overline{2}\,\overline{1}$

$\overline{18}\,\overline{7}\,\overline{3}\,\overline{10}\,\overline{12}$ $\overline{5}\,\overline{8}\,\overline{6}\,\overline{7}\,\overline{9}\,\overline{3}\,\overline{8}\,\overline{20}$

$\overline{2}\,\overline{8}$ $\overline{19}\,\overline{4}$ $\overline{3}$ $\overline{4}\,\overline{14}\,\overline{4}\,\overline{8}$ $\overline{16}\,\overline{4}\,\overline{17}\,\overline{7}$

$\overline{O}\,\overline{H}$ $\overline{3}\,\overline{10}\,\overline{4}$ $\overline{10}\,\overline{15}\,\overline{4}\,\overline{5}\,\overline{19}$ $\overline{18}\,\overline{7}\,\overline{3}\,\overline{10}\,\overline{12}\,\overline{18}$

$\overline{21}\,\overline{4}\,\overline{9}\,\overline{3}\,\overline{8}\,\overline{11}$ $\overline{18}\,\overline{2}$ $\overline{6}\,\overline{2}\,\overline{1}$ $\overline{22}\,\overline{2}\,\overline{8}\,\overline{7}{},$

$\overline{13}\,\overline{2}\,\overline{13}$ $\overline{5}\,\overline{17}\,\overline{7}\,\overline{4}\,\overline{15}$ $\overline{19}\,\overline{4}.$

$\overline{15}\,\overline{2}\,\overline{10}\,\overline{12}\,\overline{6}$ $\overline{15}\,\overline{9}\,\overline{2}\,\overline{11}\,\overline{4}\,\overline{18}$

79

Hidden Pictures
At the Pond

crescent moon

apple

flowerpot

light bulb

bell

banana

crown

mug

heart

lightning bolt

horn

raindrop

hairbrush

ring

butterfly

crayon

snake

ice-cream cone

sock

Illustrated by Laura Ferraro Close

Amuse Yourself

Ryan and three of his friends spent the day at the amusement park. Using the clues below, can you figure out what each friend's favorite ride is and what treat each ate?

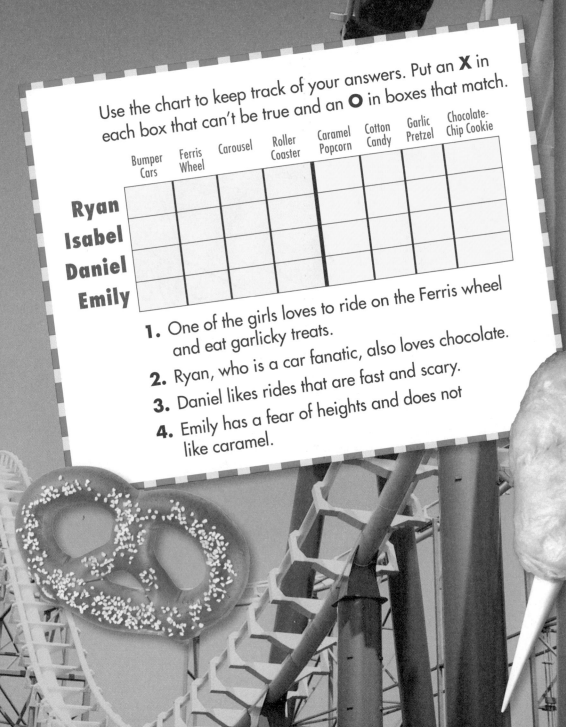

Use the chart to keep track of your answers. Put an **X** in each box that can't be true and an **O** in boxes that match.

	Bumper Cars	Ferris Wheel	Carousel	Roller Coaster	Caramel Popcorn	Cotton Candy	Garlic Pretzel	Chocolate-Chip Cookie
Ryan								
Isabel								
Daniel								
Emily								

1. One of the girls loves to ride on the Ferris wheel and eat garlicky treats.
2. Ryan, who is a car fanatic, also loves chocolate.
3. Daniel likes rides that are fast and scary.
4. Emily has a fear of heights and does not like caramel.

Puzzle by Vijayalakshmi Chary

Tree-House Boat

This tree is at sea! While everyone looks out for land, see if you can find at least **20** differences between these pictures.

Find the two houseboats above that match exactly.

On Average

Brian got to bat three times during the big game. He knocked a single, smacked a double, and walloped a triple. What was the average number of bases Brian scored during the game?

During a skating trial, three judges awarded Sylvia the scores of 8, 9, and 10. What was Sylvia's average score?

It took Terri three hours to reach Big Adventure Fun Park. She drove 40 miles in the first hour, 60 miles in the second hour, and 32 miles during the third hour. What was her average speed in miles per hour?

Illustrated by Lindy Burnett

84

Ralph went on a fishing vacation for 4 days. The first day he caught 2 fish, the second day he caught 1 fish, the third day he didn't catch any, and on the fourth, he caught 5. What was the average number of fish he caught per day?

Here is Clete's schedule for the number of movies he saw this week.

M	T	W	T	F	S	S
1	2	1	3	2	4	1

What is the average number of movies Clete saw each day during the week?

it's Fishy!

If you like to go fishing, you've come to the right puzzle.
Each fish in this aquarium has one that looks exactly like it.
Can you fish out all the matching pairs?

There is more than meets the eye at this carnival booth. Can you find the hidden objects?

kite

mitten

button

frying pan

cookie

ruler

trowel

bell

party hat

baseball

comb

horseshoe

golf club

ring

banana

snake

slice of bread

paper clip

pencil

sailboat

feather

rake

car

hockey stick

89

Camping Q's

More S'mores!

Can you help Graham find his way to the campfire to make s'mores with his friends?

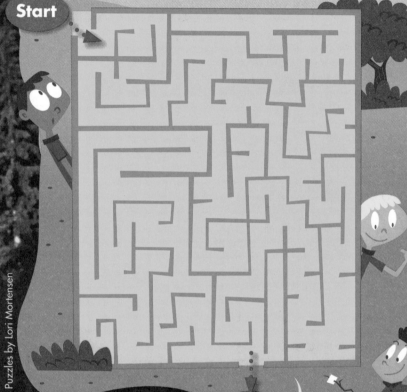

Start

Finish

Go Take a Hike!

Sticking to the trail is an important part of hiking. Which of the following are real ways of blazing or marking a trail?

A. A line of cookie crumbs

B. A sign on a tree

C. Sprinkling corn

D. A stack of rocks

E. A paint splotch on a tree

F. A pile of pinecones

Pack Pair

Can you find the two backpacks that match exactly?

Illustrated by Mike Moran, Puzzles by Lori Mortensen

Star Gazing

You've discovered a new constellation! Draw the stars, then connect the dots to show what your constellation looks like.

Parking Spaces

It's fun to camp in national parks. Can you match each national park with its state?

Yosemite
Everglades
Acadia
Grand Canyon
Big Bend
Arches

Maine
Utah
Arizona
California
Florida
Texas

JUMBLed Gear

Unscramble each set of letters to get the name of something you might bring on a camping trip.

NETT ___ ___ ___ ___

WOLPIL ___ ___ ___ ___ ___ ___

GUB SPYRA ___ ___ ___ ___ ___ ___ ___

THIGHSFALL ___ ___ ___ ___ ___ ___ ___ ___ ___ ___

PINESLEG GAB ___ ___ ___ ___ ___ ___ ___ ___
___ ___ ___

Hidden Pictures®
White Water

funnel

hamburger

pennant

pail

ladybug

loaf of bread

bow

candy cane

Hold onto your seats. The raft is entering the splash zone! Can you find the hidden objects?

fan

lock

wedge of orange

tape dispenser

mug

Illustrated by Rocky Fuller

shoe

screwdriver

comb

93

Counting Croakers

Each log can hold five frogs. Each lily pad can hold two. Will each frog here have someplace dry to rest, or will some stay in the water?

Illustrated by David Helton

Great Skate

Suki is heading to the skate park, but she needs some help figuring out which way to roll. Just one path will take her to the park. Can you help her find it?

Start

Finish

Silly Swim

Dive in carefully! There are some strange sights at the pool today. Can you find at least **25** odd, weird, or wacky things in this picture?

Illustrated by Genevieve Kote

Go for the Gold!

Twenty-five Summer Olympic sports are hiding in this grid. Look for them up, down, across, backwards, and diagonally. Be a good sport and find as many as you can.

Word List

- ~~ARCHERY~~
- BADMINTON
- BASKETBALL
- BEACH VOLLEYBALL
- CANOEING
- CYCLING
- DECATHLON
- DISCUS
- DIVING
- FENCING
- GYMNASTICS
- HANDBALL
- HIGH JUMP
- JUDO
- LONG JUMP
- MARATHON
- PENTATHLON
- SAILING
- SHOT PUT
- SOCCER
- SPRINTING
- SWIMMING
- TENNIS
- TRIATHLON
- WRESTLING

J B L B G H B B O B S L E D V
K N L H W R E S T L I N G E D
O B A F I Q A R E C C O S X D
N A B G N G C A N O E I N G I
E D T N H Y H A N D B A L L V
G M E I Q M V J T E N N I S I
N I K M P N O F U O Q U J U N
I N S M M A L M O M T O T C G
T T A I U S L A F O P R O S S
N O B W J T E R I E I A X I N
I N L S G I Y A N A H G Y D O
R V U G N C B T T O Y S R E W
P F G J O S A H I M C Y R H B
S E E I L T L O S K K H E A O
A N Q J H O L N D C E O H C A
I C U L N A Q O A U Y T R H R
L I O C Y C L I N G J P A L D
I N C S P O R T S G I U M O N
N G N G O L S T A I V T O N N
G F I G U R E S K A T I N G G

BONUS PUZZLE
We've also hidden five Winter Olympic sports in the grid. Can you find them?

Illustrated by Wendy Wax

99

Wheel Deal

Ollie's ready for a new skateboard. While he shops, jump right in and see if you can find the ten pairs of matching skateboards. When you've found them all, one board will be left. That is the one Ollie is going to buy. Can you find it?

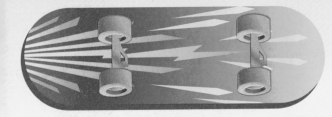

Hidden Pictures®
Sun and Sand

lock

celery

comb

vase

button

glove

banana

bat

ice pop

mushroom

slice of pizza

wedge of orange

candle

carrot

fan

crescent moon

arrow

toothpaste

fried egg

turtle

Illustrated by Mernie Gallagher-Cole

Flip for it

Chase just flipped his flying disc to his faithful friend, Otto.
Can you find the path the disc will take to reach Otto?

Finish

Start

Illustrated by Mike Moran

103

Dive In

Alex, Brooke, and Claire are competing in the big race. Who will win? Find out by answering these questions. For each question, circle the answer listed under **A**, **B**, or **C**. Then shade in the matching square in the correct swim lane. As you do, the swimmers will cruise to the finish line. Can you guess which girl will finish first?

Which is . . .

		A	B	C
1.	the fastest land animal?	tiger	rabbit	cheetah
2.	not in vanilla ice cream?	sugar	milk	flour
3.	a Midwestern state?	Minnesota	Oregon	Vermont
4.	what "arid" means?	wet	dry	cold
5.	the number of pints in a gallon?	8	16	32
6.	a woodwind instrument?	oboe	cello	tuba
7.	magenta a shade of?	yellow	orange	pink
8.	an invertebrate?	moose	snake	jellyfish
9.	the "double play" sport?	hockey	baseball	rugby
10.	mahogany a type of?	bread	wood	insect
11.	the capital of Italy?	Rome	Venice	Milan
12.	12 x 7?	78	84	96
13.	the sport that uses a "birdie"?	bowling	lacrosse	badminton
14.	a pine tree?	deciduous	coniferous	annual
15.	the shape with 10 sides?	octagon	decagon	dodecahedron
16.	a limerick a type of?	poem	dance	art
17.	a Middle Eastern country?	El Salvador	Syria	Slovakia
18.	a kind of flower?	bee's bonnet	lion's mouth	baby's breath
19.	a hairstyle?	mullet	mallet	shallot
20.	a type of olive?	yoga	kalamata	tempura

A

B

C

Puzzle by Carly Schuna

Illustrated by Garry Colby

Bike Times

Arnie, Angel, Alex, and Alisha are riding their bicycles on a 60-mile trip, all the way to Narrowsburg. Each leaves at a different time, but all of them arrive in Narrowsburg at 1 p.m. Can you tell how fast (in miles per hour) each biker pedaled? First, figure out how many hours it took each biker to reach Narrowsburg. Then divide the distance by the hours.

Arnie left at 7 a.m.
Angel left at 8 a.m.
Alex left at 9 a.m.
Alisha left at 10 a.m.

NARROWSBURG

Illustrated by Scott Peck

Gone Fishing

Brooke and three friends went fish shopping at the pet store. From the clues below, can you figure out what color fish each friend got and what tank decoration each picked out?

Use the chart to keep track of your answers. Put an **X** in each box that can't be true and an **O** in boxes that match.

	Orange	Blue	Yellow	Black	Ship	Castle	Mermaid	Coral
Brooke								
Jon								
Corinne								
Ethan								

1. Corinne's decoration is one of the two that starts with the same letter as her name.

2. The color of Ethan's fish shares three letters with his name.

3. Brooke picked out a decoration with a tower for her yellow fish.

4. The fish color and the decoration Jon picked out have the same number of letters in their names.

Hidden Pictures®
Superchallenge!

There are **30** objects hidden in this amusement park. Without clues or knowing what to look for, try to find them all. Good luck!

TICKETS

Illustrated by Paula Becker

SIR HIDE·A·LOT'S AMUSEMENT PARK

SWEET SHOPPE

FUDGE · COTTON CANDY
MILK · ICE CREAM
SODA · CANDY

River Run

Each kayaker is taking a different river to Camp Pinecone, and each is paddling at a different speed. Can you tell the order in which they will arrive at camp?

Illustrated by Bill Colrus

RIVERS	LENGTH	KAYAKERS	SPEED
White	42 miles	Noel	7 mph
Red	30 miles	Olivia	6 mph
Yellow	44 miles	Pablo	11 mph
Green	24 miles	Qan	8 mph

110

AHOY!

Come sail away with us—or row, cruise, or float. We've gathered **21** kinds of watercraft. They can fit into the grid in just one way. Use the number of letters in each word to figure out where it belongs. Write in each name and cross it off the list as you go. **Bon voyage!**

4 Letters
RAFT
SCOW

5 Letters
BARGE
CANOE
FERRY
KAYAK
SCULL
YACHT

6 Letters
DINGHY
~~JET SKI~~

7 Letters
GONDOLA
PONTOON
ROWBOAT
TUGBOAT

8 Letters
LIFEBOAT
SAILBOAT

9 Letters
CATAMARAN
HOUSEBOAT
SPEEDBOAT
STEAMBOAT

10 Letters
CRUISE SHIP

JETSKI

Take a Hike

This forest is filled with birds—you just have to take a closer look. There are **21** birds hidden in the scene. How many can you find?

Illustrated by Kevin Rechin

Hidden Pictures®
At the Pier

penguin

domino

ghost

Fishing Derby

potato

fried egg

thimble

How many fish will they catch today?
Can you find the hidden objects?

feather

acorn

butterfly

alarm clock

peanut

banana

Illustration by Marsha Winborn

Ice-Cream Q's

Truck Trail

Can you help Max and Amber catch the ice-cream truck before it leaves their block?

Start

Finish

Illustrated by Mike Moran

Puzzles by Carly Schuna

Cool Quiz

Which of these ice-cream facts are true and which are false?

1. Vanilla is the most popular ice-cream flavor in America.

   T or F

2. Neapolitan ice cream includes four flavors in the same container.

   T or F

3. People eat more ice cream in the United States than in any other country.

   T or F

4. Soft-serve ice cream is stored at room temperature.

   T or F

Gotta SPLIT

Can you find four differences between these two banana splits?

Dessert or Not?

Each pair of words has one ice-cream dessert and one faker. Circle the real desserts.

SATURDAY **or** SUNDAE?

SHERBET **or** DERVISH?

GELATO **or** LIBRETTO?

MALT **or** MOLT?

BERET **or** SORBET?

CHAMBRAY **or** PARFAIT?

A NEW Scoop

You won a contest to create your own ice-cream flavor! Draw and describe it here.

Missing Vowels

C CRM is the words ice cream with the vowels taken away. Can you identify these **C CRM** flavors?

BTTR PCN

RCKY RD

CHCLT-CHP CK DGH

CRML CRNCH

CKS ND CRM

Go Disc Golf!

It's the big disc-golf game. Everyone has just flipped a disc, but whose disc will hit a target? Follow the paths to see where each person's disc lands.

119

Pollen Path

Bee-linda wants to buzz to the flower at the center. She can fly through only five openings, and the numbers on those openings have to total 101. Can you help her find the right way to fly? Hint: The numbers 15 and 10 are in the first two openings that Bee-Linda will visit.

4
2
50
5
3
5
5
15
10
2
15
5
25
15
12
25
20
1
25
5
1
3
3
15
12
2

Sea This

This seahorse is packed with 24 things you might see under the sea. The words are hidden up, down, across, backwards, and diagonally. Take a deep breath, then dive on in!

Word List

~~CLAM~~	LOBSTER	SHRIMP
CORAL	OCTOPUS	SPONGE
CRAB	OYSTER	SQUID
DIVER	RAY	STARFISH
DOLPHIN	REEF	SUBMARINE
EEL	SCALLOP	SWORDFISH
JELLYFISH	SEA HORSE	TURTLE
KELP	SHARK	WHALE

```
                    R S
                W H A L E H Q H
            H D I U Q S E A H O R S E N
        S C A L L O P L A R O C D I V E R
                        T T O F M M U
                    Y P U O L R E P
                S A K K R P P A V O
            T S R E R B T U H T P
            O Y S T E R E L S I S H
            K G U E P T L E G N O P S
            X K E H S I F D R O W S
                S U B M A R I N E C
                O G U E K L M
        F P L E K         L B R S A
        Z L B   G S S     P A G L
        N F E             U H R C
            J E L L Y F I S H C
                R E E F
```

Hidden Pictures®
Happy 4th of July!

boomerang

comb

umbrella

toothbrush

sock

book

drinking straw

spoon

button

teacup

glove

artist's brush

cotton candy

envelope

crescent moon

Café

HAPPY 4th OF JULY

Illustrated by Sally Springer

122

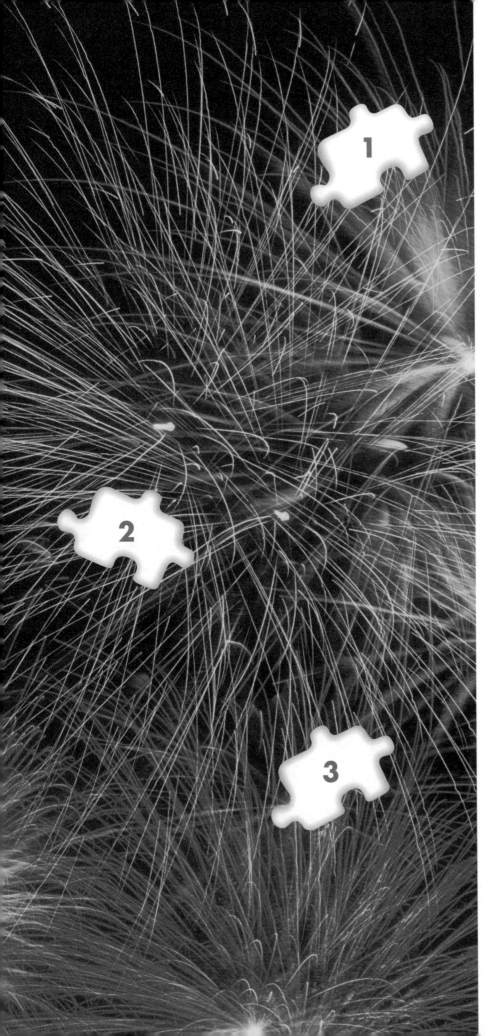

Fractured Fireworks

Which of these puzzle pieces belong in the numbered spaces?

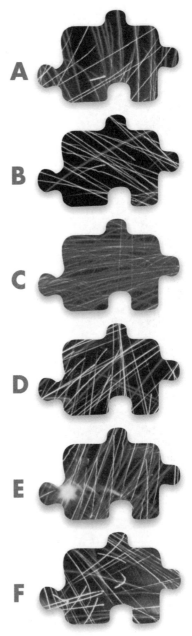

A

B

C

D

E

F

Challenge: Find where the other puzzle pieces belong.

Digit Does It

The local community center held its annual chicken roast this weekend. During the feathered festivities, the cooks collected all the wishbones that people found in the chickens. At the end of the day, when the head cook looked for the wishbones, they were gone! Luckily, that

Illustrated by Joe Boddy

intrepid investigator, Inspector Digit, was at the roast. He sprang up and grabbed this note as his first clue. Can you decode the message and help collar another crook? The first line reads **"Dear Inspector Digit."**

$$\overline{19}\ \overline{18}\ \overline{22}\ \overline{7}\quad \overline{14}\ \overline{10}\ \overline{6}\ \overline{8}\ \overline{18}\ \overline{20}\ \overline{5}\ \overline{9}\ \overline{7}\quad \overline{19}\ \overline{14}\ \overline{16}\ \overline{14}\ \overline{5}\,{}'$$

$$\overline{14}\quad \overline{20}\ \overline{15}\ \overline{9}\ \overline{13}\ \overline{18}\ \overline{19}\quad \overline{2}\ \overline{15}\ \overline{18}\ \overline{10}\quad \overline{1}\ \overline{9}\ \overline{4}$$

$$\overline{6}\ \overline{15}\ \overline{9}\ \overline{2}\ \overline{18}\ \overline{19}\quad \overline{4}\ \overline{8}\,{}'\quad \overline{21}\ \overline{4}\ \overline{5}\quad \overline{14}\ \overline{11}\quad \overline{10}\ \overline{9}$$

$$\overline{20}\ \overline{15}\ \overline{14}\ \overline{20}\ \overline{13}\ \overline{18}\ \overline{10}\,.\quad \overline{1}\ \overline{9}\ \overline{4}\quad \overline{11}\ \overline{22}\ \overline{1}\quad \overline{15}\ \overline{22}\ \overline{3}\ \overline{18}$$

$$\overline{22}\quad \overline{21}\ \overline{9}\ \overline{10}\ \overline{18}\quad \overline{5}\ \overline{9}\quad \overline{8}\ \overline{14}\ \overline{20}\ \overline{13}\quad \overline{2}\ \overline{14}\ \overline{5}\ \overline{15}$$

$$\overline{11}\ \overline{18}\,{}'\quad \overline{21}\ \overline{4}\ \overline{5}\quad \overline{14}\ \overline{17}\quad \overline{14}\quad \overline{16}\ \overline{18}\ \overline{5}\quad \overline{11}\ \overline{1}$$

$$\overline{2}\ \overline{14}\ \overline{6}\ \overline{15}\,{}'\quad \overline{22}\ \overline{12}\ \overline{12}\quad \overline{W}\ \overline{S}\quad \overline{21}\ \overline{9}\ \overline{10}\ \overline{18}\ \overline{6}$$

$$\overline{2}\ \overline{14}\ \overline{12}\ \overline{12}\quad \overline{21}\ \overline{18}\quad \overline{11}\ \overline{14}\ \overline{10}\ \overline{18}\,.$$

$$\overline{22}\ \overline{12}\ \overline{9}\ \overline{1}\ \overline{6}\ \overline{14}\ \overline{4}\ \overline{6}\quad \overline{21}\ \overline{9}\ \overline{10}\ \overline{18}\ \overline{6}$$

Tube-ular!

Come on in, the water's perfect! Before everyone rounds the bend, see if you can find at least **20** differences between these pictures.

Find the two tubes above that match exactly.

Golf Bloopers

Ready to score some fun? There are some strange sights on the mini-golf course today. Can you find at least 25 odd, weird, or wacky things in this picture?

Illustrated by Daryll Collins

Take a Bike

Maria is heading down the toughest trail in the park. Can you help her find the one path that leads to FINISH? Once you've found it, write the letters along it in order in the spaces below to answer the riddle.

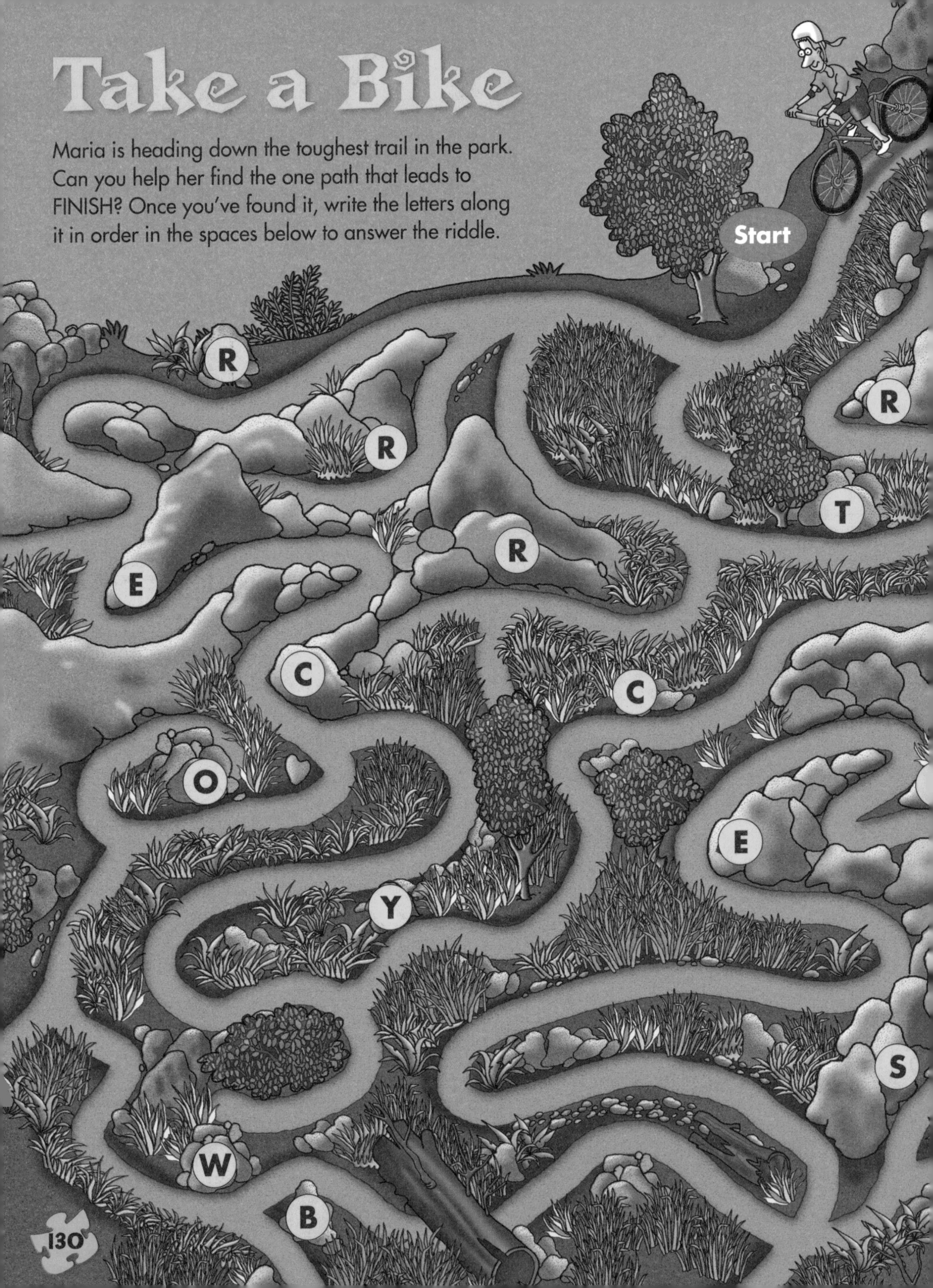

Start

R

R

R

R

T

E

C

C

O

E

Y

W

S

B

130

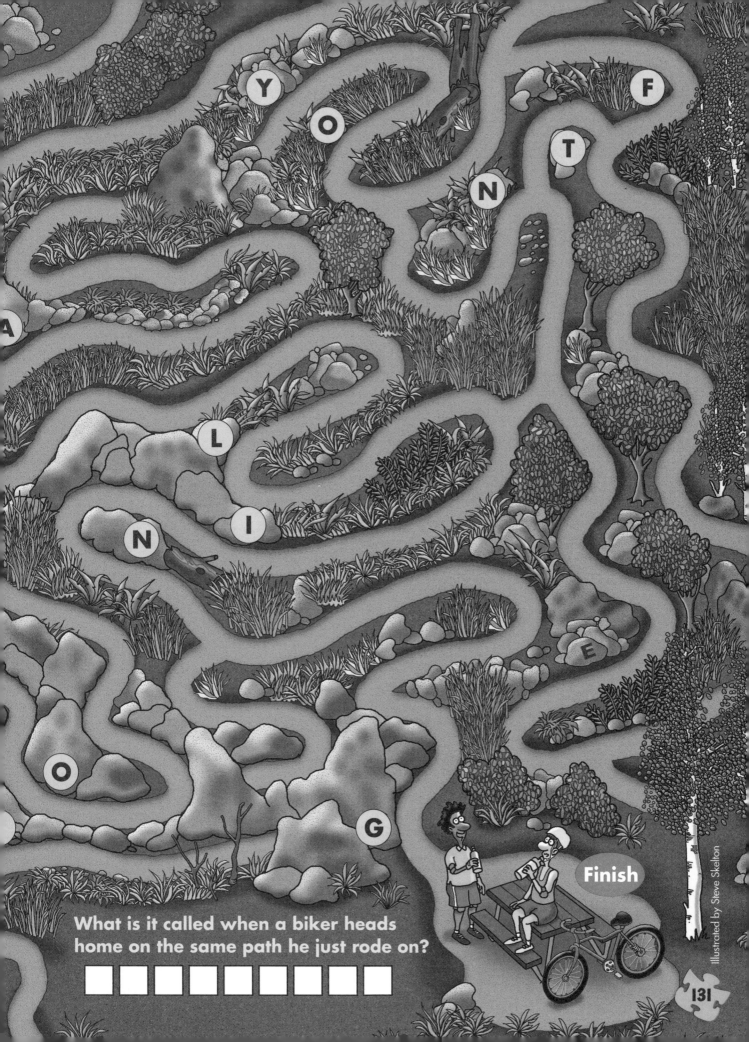

What is it called when a biker heads home on the same path he just rode on?

Hidden WORDS

There are six words (not pictures!) hidden in the scene below.
Can you find **SPLASH, SURF, SWIM, TOWEL, WAVE,** and **WET?**

Illustrated by Kelly Kennedy

5 Log Jamming

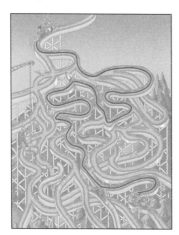

6-7 Dog Wash

8 Up the Creek

From left to right, the totals are:

Lane 1 — $3 + 5 + 9 + 1 + 7 = 25$
Lane 2 — $8 + 7 + 2 + 3 + 1 = 21$
Lane 3 — $7 + 9 + 6 + 0 + 4 = 26$
Lane 4 — $2 + 4 + 8 + 6 + 0 = 20$
Lane 5 — $2 + 1 + 3 + 5 + 4 = 15$
LANE 3 IS THE WINNER.

9 Back to the Grind

10-11 Kite Plight

13 Paddle Pals

12 Camp Out

Cole: swimming camp, August 16–31
Abby: soccer camp, August 1–15
Marissa: art camp, July 16–31
Paul: music camp, July 1–15

14-15 Ring the Bell

1. A	6. C	11. B	16. A
2. C	7. B	12. C	17. B
3. C	8. A	13. A	18. C
4. B	9. A	14. C	19. A
5. A	10. B	15. C	20. A

COLUMN A RINGS THE BELL.

Answers

16–17 Sun and Shades

18–19 Sailing Sums

White	$7 + 3 + 9 + 2 + 1 + 9 = 31$
Purple	$6 + 5 + 8 + 3 + 2 + 4 = 28$
Green	$5 + 7 + 9 + 3 + 6 + 4 = 34$
Red	$2 + 5 + 9 + 1 + 6 + 3 = 26$
Yellow	$3 + 4 + 5 + 6 + 7 + 8 = 33$
Blue	$8 + 1 + 2 + 9 + 9 + 4 = 33$

GREEN WINS!

22–23 Double Dips

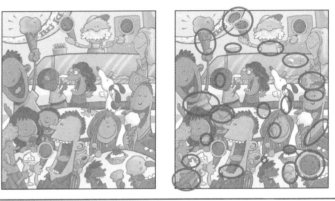

20–21 Superchallenge!

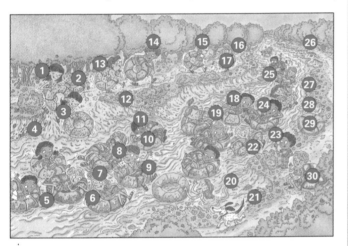

1. artist's brush
2. crown
3. pencil
4. jump rope
5. mittens
6. slice of pizza
7. dog bone
8. teacup
9. banana
10. crayon
11. mouse
12. cupcake
13. needle
14. fried egg
15. drumstick
16. scissors
17. clock
18. spoon
19. funnel
20. belt
21. heart
22. apple
23. wishbone
24. sock
25. baby's rattle
26. fish
27. candy cane
28. fork
29. football
30. doughnut

24–25 It's Campy

What do octopuses take on camping trips?

TENT-ACLES

26 This Way, Hikers!

134

27 Tic Tac Row

cherry
blue bowl
banana
spoon

whipped cream →
sprinkles →
cookie →
chocolate syrup →

30–31 Tents Up!

32 Hidden Words

28–29 Rafting Record

1. Total number of rafts needed for this group: 4
   4 guests in each of 3 rafts, and then 2 in the 4th raft

2. Total cost of the raft rental for this group: $370.00
   (3 × $105.00 = $315.00;
   2 × $27.50 = $55.00;
   $315.00 + $55.00 = $370.00)

3. Every guest is renting a paddle.
   Total number of paddles needed: 14

4. Total cost of the paddle rental for this group: $63.00
   (14 × $4.50 = $63.00)

5. Katie, Kevin, and the Kline triplets brought their own life jackets. Total cost of the life jacket rental for the rest of the group: $54.00
   (9 × $6.00 = $54.00)

6. Combined total of all charges for this group: $487.00
   ($370.00 + $63.00 + $54.00 = $487.00)

7. Total number of guides needed for this group: 4
   (same as the number of rafts)

33 Spotted Sums

Sharona will see more than 600 swallows on Monday of week 2.

34–35 Beach Q's

Beach Reach

A Shore Thing

Waikiki Beach — California
Palm Beach — Florida
Venice Beach — Hawaii
Cape Hatteras — Massachusetts
Cape Cod — North Carolina

Missing Vowels

crab
clam
sea gull
pelican
sea star

Shell Match

Jumbled Beach

ball   sandals
book   boogie board
towel   sunglasses

Answers

36 Leaping Lemonade!

37 Tic Tac Row

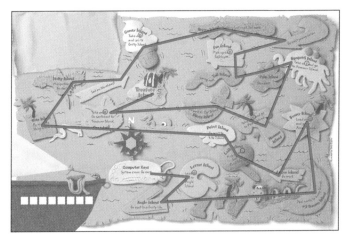

38–39 Fair Play

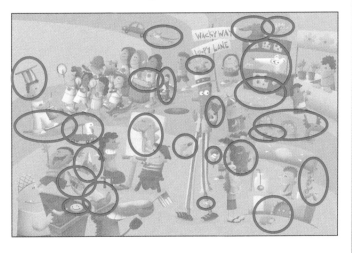

40–41 Treasure Hunt

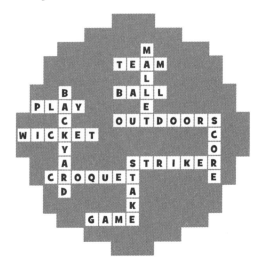

Captain Platinum's treasure is GOLDFISH.

42 Croquet Play

43 Croquet Cross

44–45 Bottled Up

What's the best place to dance at the beach?
ON A BOOGIE BOARD

46–47 Dog Days

48–49 Park Here

53 What a Catch!

50–51 Fore!

Patty	Paula	Pete	Perry
61	58	59	60

PAULA WON.

52 Moonlighting

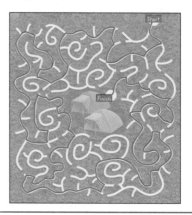

54–55 Parrot Pairs

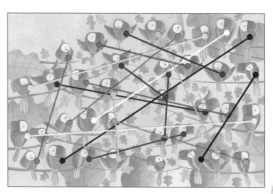

Answers

56 Grab a Board

57 Surf Cross

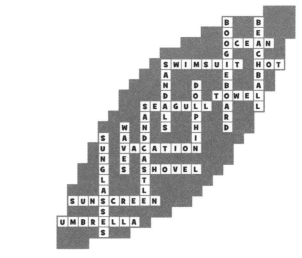

58–59 Battle of the Bands

There is no keyboard on either page.

60–61 Road Trip

WANDA'S WAY		RHONDA'S ROUTE	
START		START	
Los Angeles		Los Angeles	
San Diego	124	Las Vegas	375
Phoenix	350	Salt Lake City	486
El Paso	437	Denver	495
Amarillo	421	Oakley	253
Dallas	368	Kansas City	362
New Orleans	504	Chicago	527
Birmingham	340	Indianapolis	185
Atlanta	153	Cincinnati	110
Knoxville	219	Charleston	253
Washington, D.C.	490	Washington, D.C.	374
	3,406		3,420

Rhonda traveled more miles.

62–63 Superchallenge!

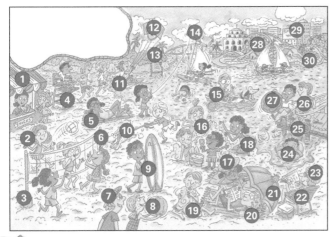

1. ladle
2. apple
3. shovel
4. book
5. artist's brush
6. pencil
7. teacup
8. crescent moon
9. safety pin
10. hoe
11. heart
12. handbag
13. glove
14. funnel
15. tennis racket
16. fried egg
17. ring
18. flower
19. snail
20. rolling pin
21. party hat
22. pizza
23. mushroom
24. hot dog
25. cane
26. fishhook
27. balloon
28. mouse
29. envelope
30. snake

Answers

64–65 Park Maze

68–69 Fork It Over

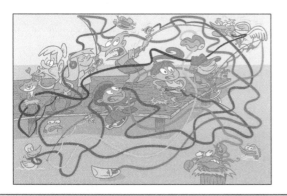

72–73 Hooked!

74 Hidden Words

66–67 Skate Q's

Get Rolling

Trick or Not?

The real tricks are:
Back Flip
Front Slide
Royale Grind
Mute Grab
Grapevine
Barrel Roll

Roller Twins

Joking Around

THE ICE MIGHT CRACK UP

Hockey or Figure?

SLAP SHOT	H	FACEOFF	H
DOUBLE AXEL	F	HAT TRICK	H
ICING	H	SALCHOW	F
TOE JUMP	F	DEATH SPIRAL	F
LUTZ	F	POWER PLAY	H

70–71 Here Comes the Sun!

75 Phone Age

Sylvia, age 14 — 802-1005
Oliver, age 15 — 521-0600
Jaime, age 7 — 233-1202
Lara, age 8 — 410-2102
Ari, age 11 — 203-0002
Bruce, age 12 — 310-0050
Lola, age 9 — 202-4000
Joel, age 16 — 614-3001
Nate, age 10 — 321-1103
Ellis, age 13 — 401-3121

139

Answers

76–77 Just Beachy

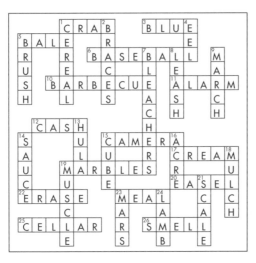

80 At the Pond

82–83 Tree-House Boat

78–79 Digit Does It

Dear Inspector Digit,

So they sent the cream of the cops after me. How sweet. But my trail will be cold before you stick anything on me. I even left 29 ice-cream sticks behind so you won't pop after me.

Rocky Rhodes

81 Amuse Yourself

Ryan: bumper cars and chocolate-chip cookie

Isabel: Ferris wheel and garlic pretzel

Daniel: roller coaster and caramel popcorn

Emily: carousel and cotton candy

84–85 On Average

Brian scored an average of 2 bases per at bat.
(six bases ÷ 3 at bats)

Sylvia's average score was 9.
(27 points ÷ 3 judges)

Terri averaged 44 miles per hour.
(132 miles ÷ three hours)

Ralph caught an average of 2 fish a day.
(8 fish ÷ 4 days)

Clete saw an average of 2 movies each day.
(14 movies ÷ 7 days)

86–87 It's Fishy!

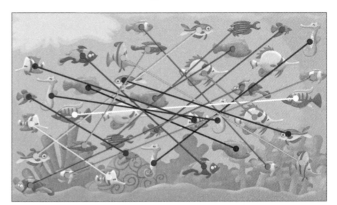

88–89 Game Plan

90-91 Camping Q's

More S'mores!

Pack Pair

Jumbled Gear
Tent, Pillow, Bug Spray, Flashlight, Sleeping Bag

Parking Spaces

Yosemite	California
Everglades	Florida
Acadia	Maine
Grand Canyon	Arizona
Big Bend	Texas
Arches	Utah

Go Take a Hike!
B, D, and E are the real ways. Over time, animals would eat the crumbs and corn, and pinecones would decompose.

92–93 White Water

94 Counting Croakers

3 logs x 5 frogs = 15 frogs

5 pads x 2 frogs = 10 frogs

15 + 10 = 25 frogs

Two frogs will be left in the water.

95 Great Skate

96–97 Silly Swim

Answers

98–99 Go for the Gold!

```
J B L B G H B B O B S L E D V
K N L H W R E S T L I N G E D
O B A F I Q A R E C C O S X D
N A B G N H C A N O E I N G I
E D T E N I G Y H A N D B A L L
G M N I Q M N V J T E N N I S U
N I M M P M U O F U O Q U J C S
I N P M U J N S M O M T O T S I
T T O M U L A L E A R F O P R O
N O N J A T I B T R I E I A X X
I N V F U G J O S A H O G Y R E
R P E Q U L T L O S K I M C H D
P S A I J H O L N D C K A U C A
S L N A Q O A U Y C R A T
I N G F O N S P O R T S G I M O N
G F N G O L S T A I V T U T
G F I G U R E S K A T I N G G
```

100–101 Wheel Deal

102 Sun and Sand

103 Flip for It

104–105 Dive In

1. c	6. a	11. a	16. a
2. c	7. c	12. b	17. b
3. a	8. c	13. c	18. c
4. b	9. b	14. b	19. a
5. a	10. b	15. b	20. b

BROOKE WINS THE RACE.

107 Gone Fishing

Brooke: yellow, castle

Jon: blue, ship

Corinne: black, coral

Ethan: orange, mermaid

106 Bike Times

Arnie biked at 10 miles an hour.

Angel biked at 12 miles an hour.

Alex biked at 15 miles an hour.

Alisha biked at 20 miles an hour.

110 River Run

Qan will arrive first in 3 hours (24 ÷ 8 = 3).

Pablo will arrive second in 4 hours (44 ÷ 11 = 4).

Olivia will arrive third in 5 hours (30 ÷ 6 = 5).

Noel will arrive fourth in 6 hours (42 ÷ 7 = 6).

108–109 Superchallenge!

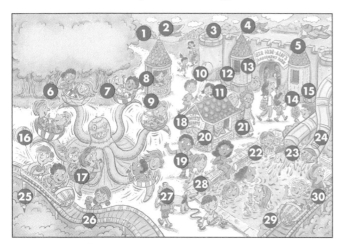

1. cupcake
2. banana
3. bow
4. boot
5. glove
6. swim fin
7. crescent moon
8. toothbrush
9. leaf
10. doughnut
11. teacup
12. baseball cap
13. ruler
14. book
15. musical note
16. ring
17. fish
18. comb
19. nail
20. pizza
21. bird
22. golf club
23. sock
24. flashlight
25. pencil
26. snake
27. fork
28. saltshaker
29. wrench
30. flute

111 Ahoy!

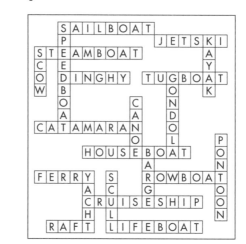

112–113 Take a Hike

114–115 At the Pier

116–117 Ice-Cream Q's

Truck Trail

Gotta Split

Cool Quiz

1. True
2. False.
   There are three
   flavors in Neapolitan.
3. True
4. False

Missing Vowels

BUTTER PECAN
ROCKY ROAD
CHOCOLATE-CHIP
 COOKIE DOUGH
CARAMEL CRUNCH
COOKIES AND CREAM

Dessert or Not?

SUNDAE
SHERBET
GELATO
MALT
SORBET
PARFAIT

Answers

118–119 Go Disc Golf!

120 Pollen Path

Here is our answer. May-bee you found another.

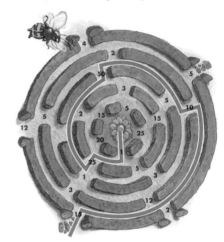

121 Sea This

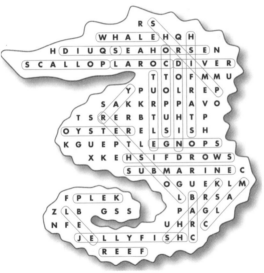

122 Happy 4th of July!

123 Fractured Fireworks

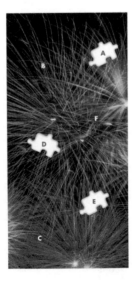

124–125 Digit Does It

Dear Inspector Digit,

I choked when you showed up, but I'm no chicken. You may have a bone to pick with me, but if I get my wish, all 26 bones will be mine.

Aloysius Bones